please
READ
THIS FIRST

Guidance:

As this is a Sacred Work, please approach it with reverence.

The LIGHT within this book WILL 'Begin' or 'Accelerate' your Evolution.

Do NOT open this book unless you are ready to take responsibility for Your Own Evolution or what this LIGHT might open within your life.

It is suggested, the first time you open this book, read it slowly, as a meditation, and read it in one sitting.

You will need around half an hour.

For Janet.

VISION

Blessings
and

Peace

corpio /851

VISION

a sacred text

VISION

was given to the author in a Flash of Insight
after responding to a call from an ancient Sacred Site
in Wales in November 2006

The

UNIVERSAL PLAN

is

IN SIGHT

Act I

In the
BEGINNING

There

was

TIME

... and

the

ENLIGHTENED

ONES

came to

TEACH US

...but

few

LISTENED

and

EVEN FEWER

HEARD

Then

TIME

began to

RUN OUT

... and

nobody

PERCEIVED

the

WAVE *of* TIME

... and

nobody

heard

THE CALL

... and

nobody

had

THE VISION

... even

though

THE CALLING

had

BEGUN

And

nobody

SAW

the

JOURNEY

... even

though

THE MANY

were already

TRAILING BEHIND

And

the

WAVE *of* TIME

began to

ACCELERATE

… as

the

MAYA PROPHESIED

with their
CALENDAR
of
TIME

And

then there was

NO TIME

to

LOSE

... but

nobody realised

TIME

was

RUNNING OUT

And

GOD

was

AMAZED

at the

BLINDNESS *of* HUMANS

Why

could they not

SEE

HIS VISION

of

THE JOURNEY?

... for

nobody with

EYES

could fail to

SEE

... and

nobody with

INSIGHT

could fail to

SEE

... and

nobody with

LOVE

could fail to

SEE

Where

GOD

had placed this

VISION

of

HIS JOURNEY

But

FAIL *they* DID

and

BLIND *they* ARE

And

NOW

TODAY

There is

NO
TIME!

Act II

The

EXPANDING

Breath *of* Life

BANG

●

God Takes a Breath

The Universe Expands

The

EXPANDING

●

UNIVERSE

IS

...the

IN-BREATH

of

G●D

As

G●D

breathes in

●

THE UNIVERSE

EXPANDS

As

Y●U

breathe in

●

YOUR LUNGS

E X P A N D

Take

a

DEEP

BREATH

Notice:

as you

BREATHE IN

your breath

SPEEDS UP

Notice:

THE UNIVERSE

IS

SPEEDING UP

Notice:

the

EXPANSION

of your lungs reaches a

LIMIT

The

EXPANSION

of the

UNIVERSE

is reaching its

LIMIT

The

EARTH

is in the

ASCENSION

PHASE

We

are all

ASCENDING

to the year

2012

The

IN-BREATH

of

G●D

is almost

COMPLETE

There

is

NO TIME

to

LOSE

In

AWAKENING

to

CHANGE

Act III

The

CONNECTING

Thread *of* Life

BANG

Consciousness Expands

From

the CORE *of*

●

all

THAT IS

... the

MIND

of

G●D

EXPANDS

Every

ATOM

●

in

THE UNIVERSE

Contains

the

MIND

of

G ● D

You

are made of

A T ● M S

You

are always

ATTACHED

●

to the

CORE

You

are always

CONNECTED

●

to

UNITY

By

the

●

THREAD *of* LIFE

...which

is

●

UNIVERSAL

CONSCIOUSNESS

Act iV

The

ILLUSION

•

BANG

Threads are Everywhere

You

are

N ● T

S E P A R A T E

This

is only

I L L U S I O N

Illusion

fills you with

SENSE *of* SELF

You

are

N ● T

your

S E L F

You

are filled with

EGO-SELF

Becoming

EMPTY

of

EGO-SELF

Will

REVEAL

●

your

REAL SELF

Then

you will

EXPERIENCE

... you

are

N ● T

S E P A R A T E

... but

CONNECTED

to the

●

CORE

of all

THAT IS

By

the

●

Thread *of* Life

Imagine

you are

CONNECTED

●

by

E-L-A-S-T-I-C

When

E - L - A - S - T - I - C

reaches its

●

limit of

EXPANSION

You

are

COMPELLED

●

TO RETURN

to the

POINT *of* ORIGIN

... you

are

COMPELLED

●

TO RETURN

to the

CORE

... you

are

COMPELLED

●

TO RETURN

to

U N I T Y

A*ct* V

Hark

a NAME *is*

CALLED

Through

many lifetimes you have

JOURNEYED

●

from the

C O R E

You

have reached the

LIMIT

of your

EXPANSION

INTO

SEPARATION

The

CORE

●

CONSCIOUSNESS

is now

CALLING

It

is

CALLING

your

NAME

It

is

CALLING

in your

HEART

It

is

CALLING

YOU

to

TURN

If

you are looking at this page

then

YOUR NAME

has been

C A L L E D

BELIEVE

●

IT

Your

NAME

has been

CALLED

...from

the

●

C O R E

of all

T H A T   I S

For

it is your time to

E N T E R

●

the LIGHT *of*

A Q U A R I U S

To

begin the

JOURNEY

●

towards

UNITY

The

FIRST STEPS

of

ILLUMINATION

You

are now beginning the

J O U R N E Y

●

towards

H O M E

Your

H E A R T

is responding

to the

C A L L

Each step

you take will

BRING

●

AWAKENING

Each Step

you take will

B R I N G

E V O L U T I O N

Each Step

you take will

B R I N G

●

L O V E

... into

YOUR

●

HEART

... into

YOUR

●

L I F E

... into

YOUR

●

WORLD

You

are

BECOMING

●

ILLUMINATED

By

the

LIGHT *of* LOVE

●

from the

CORE

The

D O O R

●

is

O P E N

Your

only

LIMITATION

is your

S E L F

The

F I R S T

have been

C A L L E D

The

COLLECTIVE
CONSCIOUSNESS

is the

CONSCIOUSNESS

of the

MASSES

The

COLLECTIVE
CONSCIOUSNESS

is still

EXPANDING

into

SEPARATION

... still

SEPARATING

●

from

UNITY

The

CALLING

to return to

●

UNITY

HAS BEGUN

Each

in their

T U R N

will be

CALLED

As

their

H E A R T S

are ready for

ILLUMINATION

Many

have already been

CALLED

Called

for their

INNER

STRENGTH

Called

to

LEAD *and* GUIDE

those who are

AWAKENING

Called

for their

COURAGE

to swim against the

FLOW

Of
the
OUTPOURING

into

SEPARATION

Called

to

S W I M

against the

F L O W

Of
the
COLLECTIVE
CONSCIOUSNESS

of the

MASSES

Called

from the

ILLUSION *of* SEPARATION

towards the

TRUTH *of* UNITY

Out of
ILLUSION
and into
TRUTH

As

you learn to

S W I M

against the

F L O W

Your

PERCEPTIONS

CHANGE

You

begin to

SEE

DIFFERENTLY

You

begin to

SEE

DEEPER

You

begin to

SEE

TRUTH

As

you learn to

AWAKEN

to your own

TRUTH

The

FIRE *of* LOVE

begins to

BURN *in your* HEART

As

you begin to

PERCEIVE

your own

TRUTH

You

become

COMPELLED

to follow that

TRUTH

As

you step into

YOUR

TRUTH

... life

can become

DIFFICULT

… relationships

can become

DIFFICULT

...friendships

can become

DIFFICULT

You

may become

O U T *of* S T E P

with those around

Y O U

As

you are

P U L L E D

against the

F L O W

As

you are

P U L L E D

out of

I L L U S I O N

And

into

●

T R U T H

… then

you are

BECOMING

The

●

SPIRITUAL WARRIOR

The

WARRIOR

of

TRUTH

The

ENLIGHTENED

●

ONE

LEARNING
to
TRUST

Ability

to see

T R U T H

●

at first can be

DIFFICULT

As

you awaken…

CHAOS

can

ENSUE

You

may become

CHALLENGED

CHALLENGED

to change

YOUR

LIFE

CHALLENGED

to listen to

YOUR

HEART

CHALLENGED

to follow

●

TRUTH

YOUR

•

TRUTH

The

biggest

CHALLENGE

will be

T R U S T

LEARNING

to

TRUST

your

HEART

LEARNING

to

TRUST

your

FEELINGS

LEARNING

to

TRUST

●

your

TRUTH

...and

LEARNING

to

ACCEPT

you have been

CALLED

To

AWAKEN

into

TRUTH

Act X

The

ONE VERSE

There

is no

M A P

for this

J O U R N E Y

Yet

few can make this

●

JOURNEY

ALONE

At

times you will get

LOST

and

CONFUSED

… then
you must observe
THE LAWS

of the

UNIVERSE

The

•

U N I

V E R S E

The

●

ONE VERSE
of
EVOLUTION

The

FIRST LAW

IS

You

cannot walk this

PATH

ALONE

The

SECOND LAW

IS

You

must learn to

REACH OUT

for

H E L P

When

you are

LOST or CONFUSED

you must

REACH OUT

…for
the
UNIVERSAL PLAN

is to
COME
TOGETHER

To

UPLIFT

EACH

OTHER

To

ASSIST

EACH

OTHER

To

RE - TURN

●

to

UNITY

...for

we are

N ● T

SEPARATE

... and

few can make this

●

JOURNEY

A L O N E

When

you

UPLIFT

O T H E R S

... you

BECOME

UPLIFTED

your

S E L F

Then

YOU KNOW

YOU

are not

SEPARATE

... and

YOU KNOW

you cannot make

YOUR JOURNEY

ALONE

LEARN

to

REACH OUT

The

JOURNEY

may be many

LIFETIMES

Perhaps
you can make it

in

O N E

At times

you may need

GUIDING

When

you learn to

REACH OUT

you will meet a

GUIDE

You
will meet some
ONE

●

with the answer

YOU SEEK

They

will be

●

HEAVEN

SENT

You

will be given

LESSONS

to help you find your

P A T H

As
you
L E A R N
so the

I N N E R
E X P A N S I O N
begins

As

you

L E A R N

so the

I N N E R
V I S I O N

expands

As
you
L E A R N
your

GIFTS &
TALENTS
unfold

You

will become

EMPOWERED

●

from the

C O R E

Every
lesson
LEARNED

will be

REWARDED

To

SEE &

UNDERSTAND

the

LESSONS

You

may need a

●

GUIDE

LEARN

to

REACH OUT

for

HELP

LEARN

to

REACH OUT

for

GUIDANCE

LEARN

to

REACH OUT

for

LOVE

LEARN

to

REACH INWARDS

for

LOVE

… for

few can make this

●

JOURNEY

ALONE

Act XII

The

JOURNEY

is

INSIGHT

The
journey of
EVOLUTION

is a two-way

JOURNEY

Of

OUTER

&

INNER

EXPANSION

The

EXPANSION

of

CONSCIOUSNESS

The

JOURNEY

has always been

●

IN

SIGHT

The

trick is

LEARNING

to

S E E

The

hearts and minds of

THE MASSES

will not yet

S E E

Until
they
TURN

from

SEPARATION

Towards

●

UNITY

Until

they

O P E N

their

H E A R T S

...until
they
SURRENDER

to the

CALL

...until
they

LEARN

how to

SEE

The
JOURNEY
towards
SEPARATION

is

LIMITATION

The

JOURNEY

towards

UNITY

●

is

EXPANSION

Those

continuing to choose

S E P A R A T I O N

experience

L A C K *of* V I S I O N

LACK

of

INNER VISION

LACK

of

INSIGHT

Yet

THE
JOURNEY

has always been

IN SIGHT

The
VISION
of
THE JOURNEY

SEPARATION

BEGINS *to* SEEK

•

UNITY

There

is only one

J O U R N E Y

●

everything else is

I L L U S I O N

The

JOURNEY

●

IS

The

EVOLUTION

of

HUMAN

CONSCIOUSNESS

As

you

TURN

●

towards

UNITY

Your

H E A R T

●

will begin to

O P E N

Then

you will

SEE

●

THE PATH

CLEARLY

As

you

OPEN

●

your

EYES

And

LOOK

●

with your

HEART

Then

you will

●

TRULY

SEE

With

●

INSIGHT

And

with

INSIGHT

then you will

TRULY SEE

Where

GOD

●

PLACED HIS VISION

of

THE JOURNEY

The

VISION

IS

And

THE END

IS

...just

The

BEGINNING

The

JOURNEY

BEGINS

at

www.thevisionjourney.com

This book is numbered

319

Published by Crucible Publishers
Norton St Philip Bath BA2 7LA UK
e-mail: sales@cruciblepublishers.com
www.cruciblepublishers.com

1 3 5 7 9 0 8 6 4 2

Vision was originally published in a handmade edition of
thirteen copies by Bracketpress, England, August 2007
www.bracketpress.co.uk

This edition set in Stemple Garamond

Typeset by Christian Brett

ISBN 978-1-902733-11-1

Printed in Croatia by Zrinski, Čakovec